Dear readers,

Thanks so much for reading this edition of Outhouse Books. In this edition, we present unique anecdotes about everyone's favorite holiday, Halloween.

Hopefully you enjoy this brand of specialized reader. It is designed for those of you who like to have a sense of accomplishment, but have limited time to read. These quick readers can be completed in one session….even in the privacy of your own "outhouse."

We hope you enjoy! Happy reading!!!

Sincerely,
The Outhouse Staff

Outhouse Books

Summary: A collection of interesting facts, trivia, and tidbits about Halloween.
Author: Christopher Forest
Editor: Melissa Forest

ISBN-13: 978-1480013995
Outhouse Books
Danvers, MA 01923
1 2 3 4 5 6 7 8 9 0 1

HALLOWEEN ORIGINS

Halloween originated mainly from the pagan holiday of Samhain (and, for those of you who are new to the term, it is pronounced Sow-win). This night marked the Druid new year. The real world and spirit world were thought to be closely connected during this time of year.

Samhain meant "summer's end." It was marked with harvest celebrations and large bonfires to commemorate the oncoming disappearance of the sun during winter.

Druids who celebrated Samhain believed that spirits roamed the countryside during October 31. Because some spirits might be friskier than others, Druids typically feared the night.

Masquerading??? The Druids often wore masks on October 31. This was a way to confuse any evil spirits who might be looking to frighten a passerby. The spirits themselves would be confused and perhaps look for someone else to haunt.

If Charlie Brown™ was fearful of Halloween, he wouldn't have pentaphobia....he'd have Samhainophobia, or the intense fear of all things Halloween.

During Samhain, the Druids would build a communal bonfire and extinguish all existing fires in their houses and villages. They would start the new year by creating this new bonfire. Community members would then light their own home fires from the community bonfire.

Clan of the cave cat? Irish Druids would often gather near Oweynegat, a cave that means "Cave of the Cat." It was hear that, the goddess of war, was said to emerge each year.

Druids of Scotland believed that a child born on the night of Samhain had special powers. Among these powers was the power of divination, which might make them able to predict the future.

In the early 600s, boosted by the efforts of Pope Gregory, pagan holidays like Samhain were eradicated and replaced with similar Christian ones. All Hallow's Eve developed from these efforts.

All Hallow's Eve marked the day before the Christian holiday to remember the dead who were waiting to go to heaven. It is followed by All Saint's Day (November 1) and then All Soul's Day (November 2). For Christians, All Hallow's Eve took the place of Samhain, which was celebrated from October 31- November 1.

HALLOWEEN SUPERSTITIONS

Spider man! An old custom claims that on Halloween it is good luck to see a spider.

Mirror, mirror! According to legend, Halloween night is when the real world and spirit world meet. On this night, many customs were used in Europe to help a woman predict her future husband. In Scandinavian countries, women were encouraged to look in a mirror on Halloween night. The face of her future husband sometimes stared back.

In Scotland, it was customary for unmarried women to peel an apple on Halloween. They would try to peel the apples as whole as possible and toss the apple peel over their shoulders. The peels were believed to take the form of the initial of their future husbands.

In Ireland, people used to eat barnbrack (or barmbrack) cake on Halloween night. The sweetbread contained three items hidden inside to help predict a person's future in the year ahead. A person who found a ring hidden in his or her piece was going to be married (or if already married, be happy) in the year ahead. A person who found a coin might have a prosperous year ahead. Alas, a person who found a rag in his or her piece of cake might need it later to rub their eyes. His or her year ahead was going to be less than prosperous.

In Ireland, Irish unmarried lasses (and lads) would sometimes cut a piece of their hair and place it in the Halloween bonfire. It was often believed that the person would later dream about their future spouse.

According to superstition, ancient Irish Celts believed that goblins and fairies roamed the countryside on Halloween. They would often try to gather people up to imprison them. People were encouraged to through dust on any create resembling a fairy or goblin to make them close their eyes. That way, any prisoners could flee.

Superstitious Celtic farmers thought spirits might try to harm animals on Halloween. If the farmer suspected an animal may have been tampered with, there was a simple cure – spit on your animal.

Some ancient Europeans believed that if a woman ate a food made of hazelnut, nutmeg, and walnuts before bed on Halloween, she would dream of her future husband. There is no record of what would happen if a woman had a nightmare instead.

As easy as Snap Apple! Snap Apple was a popular game in old Ireland, particularly on Halloween. Played by dangling an apple from a string tied to a ceiling, revelers would try to take a bit out of the apple blindfolded. The first person to get a bite won the privilege of eating the entire apple….good thinking. This custom led to the modern custom of bobbing for apples.

Watch where you're going! According to ancient superstition, a person can guarantee that he or she will see a witch if he or she wears clothes inside out and then walks backwards on Halloween.

In Scotland, on Halloween night, would-be brides hoping to find a husband would write the name of a suitor on a hazel nut. Once she placed all possible suitors' names on nuts, she would cast the nut into the fire. The nut that did not pop, but rather burned to ashes, showed the name of the future husband (later, it was believed that the name that burned represented a love that would not last).

Brrrrr! During some ancient Halloween parties, people would eat chestnuts. The first unmarried person who found a burr in their chestnut would marry. Wonder who came up with that idea?

What are your favorite Halloween
memories? Write them here for posterity.

_____

_____

_____

_____

_____

_____

_____

_____

_____

_____

_____

_____

_____

_____

HALLOWEEN ECONOMICS

You want to be the Halloween king of your neighborhood. Unless you give out those huge candy bars – you know how every neighborhood has the one house that gives out the King Size Bars – then your best bet is Snickers™. It is the preferred treat of most trick-or-treaters (and their parents, too).

Talk about commercial. The most commercially successful holiday each year is Christmas. But number two on that list is Halloween. It's no wonder why Halloween decorations go on sale in August! In America alone, people spend 6.8 billion dollars on the holiday.

The top five most bought candies at Halloween are candy corn, Snickers™, Reese's Peanut Butter Cups™, Kit Kats™, and M&M's™ (the ones in the small bags, of course).

North Americans eat 20 million pounds of candy corn each year…..it is the most popular candy to buy (though not to give) at Halloween.

The top selling candies on Halloween are chocolates ones. Americans spend about 1.2 billion on chocolate each year. In comparison, non-chocolates rake in about 880 million each year.

According to some surveys, the top three days to buy Halloween candy in America are October 28, followed by October 27 and October 30.

Are you typical? The average American spends about $44 on Halloween candy each year. No one is too sure much of that is spent on candy for the trick-or-treaters and how much is spent on individuals who dip into the extras.

In the United States, Americans spend about $1.65 billion on Halloween decorations.

Want to be the least popular candy giver on your block....then give away those weird taffy candy items that come in mixed candy bags. Those typically are voted the least desirable Halloween candy by trick-or-treaters.

North Americans spend more than $3 billion a year on Halloween costumes.

Season's Greetings. Make sure you do like Linus and send out your Great Pumpkin cards this year. Halloween has turned into a greeting card business. In 2009, at least 35 million Halloween cards were sent.

For those Reese's Peanut Butter™ cup lovers out there, if you want to have the best chance to get a peanut butter cup, then you better head to a two story house. Your chances are 26% better to get the holy grail of candy there than at a ranch house.

Tootsie Rolls were the first tiny candy to be individually wrapped...it made it perfect for early trick-or-treaters.

HALLOWEEN WORD MAKER

How many words can you make from the word Jack O
Lantern ….list them below

HALLOWEEN CUSTOMS

Trick-or-treating is thought to date back to the Middle Ages in Europe. There, people would go door to door asking for soul-cakes for food. In return, the people would promise to say a prayer for the giver's departed family members. Every soul cake eaten (after the prayer of course) meant another soul saved.

The following is a popular soul caking song from long ago...

Soul, soul, an apple or two
If you haven't an apple, a pear will do
One for Peter, two for Paul
Three for the Man who made us all.

In ancient times, it was believed that witches held two festivals– or sabbats – on Halloween night. Incidentally, the word witch comes from "wicca" which means "wise woman."

The idea and custom of trick-or-treating has existed for some time. However, the first mention of it in North American print occurred in 1927. The term was used in an article published in Blackie, Alberta, Canada.

As a way to celebrate the life of others who went on to the other world, people who celebrated Halloween long ago often brought food, such as fruit or cakes, to their beloved departed. It may have given rise to some versions of the Day of the Dead ceremony in South America.

Check Your Charlie Brown™ Knowledge

See if you can answer these five questions
based on
It's the Great Pumpkin Charlie Brown ™

1. What does Linus have in his hand when
he jumps into Charlie Brown's pile of
leaves?

2. Why does Charlie Brown think Lucy will
hold the football when he tries to kick it?

3. What did Charlie Brown have "a little
trouble with," when preparing his costume?

4. Why was Charlie Brown needed as a
model at Violet's Halloween party?

5. What song makes Snoopy cry at the same
party?

Check Your Charlie Brown Knowledge Answers

1. Linus has a wet sucker (or giant lollipop) when he jumps into the pile of leaves.

2. Lucy gives Charlie Brown a signed document saying she won't pull the football away. Later she does because it was "not properly notarized."

3. Scissors

4. Charlie Brown's head (in particular the back of it) is needed to design a jack o' lantern.

5. Snoopy cries at Schroeder's rendition of "It's A Long Way to Tipperary."

The ancient Romans celebrated a similar holiday to Halloween called Pomona. It celebrated the harvest goddess of the same name. Interestingly, the Romans played a version of bobbing for apples.

Ancient Celts often threw cow bones on their large fires right before Halloween. They believed that this would help ensure the sun would return the following spring. As a result, the fires were known as "bonefires" to some…..now known as bonfires.

In the Middle Ages, people often dressed up in costumes, particularly those connected to biblical figures, and would roam towns around Halloween time. They would often tell biblical stories, as well as myths, in costume. This idea of mumming helped inspire the idea of modern trick-or-treating with disguises.

HALLOWEEN SONGS

According to Billboard, the following are a handful of the top Halloween songs of all time.

5. *Highway to Hell* by ACDC

4. *Werewolves of London* by Warren Zevon

3. *Ghostbusters* by Ray Parker Junior

2. *Monster Mash* by Bobby Pickett and the Crypt Kickers

1. *Thriller* by Michael Jackson

HALLOWEEN AROUND THE WORLD

Some parts of the world, such as France and Australia, have not fully adopted the trick-or-treating tradition. They view it as an overly American commercial influence.

Yue Lan is the name of the festivals celebrated on Halloween in Hong Kong. Translated into the "festival of the hungry ghosts", celebrators appease any angry ghosts that might roam that night. Lanterns are lit and food is left to keep these pesky spirits away.

Many parts of South America, in particular Brazil, celebrate the Day of the Dead around Halloween. It is a day to remember the deceased and includes visits to graveyards. Some people view it as a somber holiday.

In China, people celebrate Halloween with a *Teng Chieh,* or Lantern Festival. Lanterns, in the shapes of dragons, are set up on streets and help guide ancestors back to their homes. There, food and water is waiting for the spirits.

In England, the British have their own celebration near Halloween, which has helped establish the trick-or-treat tradion. On November 5, the British celebrate Guy Fawkes Day in commemoration of the execution of Guy Fawkes, whose plot to blow up the parliament building and overthrow King James I in 1605 was thwarted. In the 1800s, children used to go out to the streets and beg a passersby for a "penny for the Guy."

Halloween Jokes

1. Why couldn't the skeleton knock on the door for trick or treats?
 He didn't have the guts.

2. What do ghosts eat for breakfast on Halloween morning?
 Scream of Wheat and Rice Creepers

3. Why can't witches get angry when they are on their brooms?
 They don't want to fly off the handle.

4. Why don't mummies make good friends to trick or treat with?
 They are too wrapped up in themselves.

5. What do you give a vampire with a cold?
 Coffin drops.

Owls are often associated with Halloween. It was once believed that witches could turn themselves into owls. Old-timers believed that to hear the owl's call on Halloween was a sign that someone was going to die.

Black has become a traditional Halloween color for a simple reason…it was associated with death, as was the holiday. As for orange, many of the fruits and vegetables that ripened at harvest time were….orange.

You've got Jack! The custom of carving a Jack-O-Lantern comes from Ireland. There, people believed that a dastardly man named Jack passed away. He was too wicked to go to heaven, but he had cheated the devil so many times, that he couldn't go to hell either. Believe or not, that old devil actually felt pity for Jack. He gave jack a glowing coal to put in a carved turnip and Jack was set to wander earth. He eventually got the name Jack of the Lantern, which has been transformed to Jack O'Lantern.

Skeletons became part of the Halloween symbolism because skulls and bones were early symbols of death in many religions.

Scarecrows have slowly been connected to Halloween based on the idea that Halloween helped celebrate the harvest. Scarecrows protected the harvest – and off course had those scary faces - hence the connection.

Meow! The idea of associating black cats with Halloween dates back to the Middle Ages. At a time when the belief in the supernatural and witchcraft were prevalent, some people believed that witches could escape detection by changing in a cat. Black cats were naturally more mysterious for their coloring, hence the connection to Halloween.

Some face. In Ireland, turnips and potatoes were carved with eerie faces and put in windows to keep away spirits. In England, large beets replace turnips and potatoes for the same purpose. When the custom came to America, the native and more common pumpkin was used to illuminate the light and scare away spirits. This is how the Halloween custom of the jack-o-lantern began.

Yum. The traditional food of Ireland on Halloween night was Colcannon. This was a mix of foods harvested at the time. It is made by mixing kale with mashed potatoes and placing it on raw onions. Usually, colcannon is served with boiled ham or Irish bacon.

Vampire bats are part of Halloween lore....but they are not from Transylvania. They are blood drinking bats from Central and South America. They often lap their blood, and do not suck it.

PUMPKINS

Large melons! The word pumpkin comes from the ancient Greek word, "pepon," which means large melon. Pumpkins might not be a true melon, but they are classified as a fruit.

Pumpkins were first developed by Native American cultures in the Central American regions.

Want to see the Great Pumpkin? Well, if you are like Linus then head to Illinois. There, you will find the most sincere pumpkin patches in the country. It provides more than 90 percent of the pumpkins in the United States each year. California, New York, and Ohio also produce a lot of pumpkins as well.

Want to grow your own pumpkin. Well,
follow these steps:

1. Save your pumpkin seeds from the
   prior year.
2. Plant between the last week in May
   and mid-June.
3. Water and care for them for 90-120
   days.
4. They are ready to pick when they are
   bright orange in October.

The largest pumpkins are able to grow up to 40 pounds a day when they add most of their weight….and incidentally, most of their weight is water.

Pumpkin flowers! The yellow flowers you see sprout from many pumpkin vines are just as edible as the pumpkin themselves. Tastes like chicken….well maybe not. Just make sure the flowers are safe and don't have a disease. Then, find and follow a recipe to serve them.

They aren't just orange…..pumpkins actually come in blue, green, and white varieties. Check one out for your next Halloween pumpkin.

Many county fairs share the largest pumpkin grown in their region.

Are pumpkins healthy???

Yes they are!
1. They are low in fat, sodium, and calories.
2. They are a good source of vitamins A and B, as well as potassium and iron.
3. They are high in fiber.
4. They are a source of protein.

HALLOWEEN AMERICAN STYLE

The Pilgrims were the first Americans known to hold a feast day during Halloween time. Having only been 15 years removed from Guy Fawkes attempt to overthrow the government, they celebrated Guy Fawkes Day in Plymouth. However, as America slowly evolved into its own identity, the idea of celebrating Guy Fawkes Day diminished.

The middle and southern colonies of colonial America held early versions of Halloween parties around October 31. During the time, a celebration to honor the harvest was held. People in those colonies put on plays and even told ghost stories to celebrate the middle of fall. As illustrated in Washington Irving's tale *Legend of Sleepy Hollow*, fortune telling, dancing and song were popular at the time.

The ideas of celebrating Halloween with jack-o-lanterns, first came to the United States in 1840, when Irish immigrants arrived in America to flee the potato famine. It has grown slowly ever since. In the early 1900s, Irish and Scottish communities began re-establishing the ideas of guising (dressing in masks) and souling (going door to door).

Trick or treating gained popularity in the United States in the 1930s, in part as a way to diminish youth causing mischief on Halloween night. In fact, the country's first mass-produced costumes appeared in stores in the 1930s and organized trick-or-treating began in many cities.

Go east young man! The custom of trick-or-treating gained popularity first in the western part of the United States, including California, and traveled east.

Sugar rush! In the 1940s, trick-or-treating toned down in many parts of the United States. This is due mainly to the fact that there was sugar rationing as a result of World War II. In fact, the idea of trick-or-treating became much less common between 1942 and 1947. Instead, communities hosted Halloween parties and people attended these parties with donations for the war effort.

Following World War II, the 1950s and 1960s saw trick-or-treating revived and expanded to the custom we see today, complete with popular icons turned out in costumes.

Halloween Capital of the East Coast

The city of Salem, Massachusetts has declared itself one of the Halloween capitals of the United States. It's long standing connection to the infamous witch trials (although the people involved were from nearby Danvers), it tourist attractions, and its current status as a haven for modern day witches has made it a place where people flock every October.

Halloween Capital of the West Coast

The United States has a second Halloween capital and this one is located closer to the west coast. It is the city of Anoka, Minnesota. It is believed that the first Halloween celebration in the country occurred here in 1920. The U.S. Congress actually gave it the official title of Halloween Capital of the World in 1937.

New York City holds the largest Halloween parade in the country. More than 2 million people flock to the city to watch the parade each year.

Great Towns to Live In For Halloween

- Candy Town, Ohio
- Cape Fear, North Carolina
- Frankenstein, Missouri
- Pumpkin Bend, Arkansas
- Pumpkin Hollow, New York
- Scary, West Virginia
- Spook City, Colorado.
- Tombstone, Arizona
- Witch Hazel, Oregon

Trick-or-treating came into vogue in United States cartoons in the 1950s. In 1951, Charles Schulz mentions it in a memorable *Peanuts* ™strip. And, the following year, Walt Disney productions put out a classic Donald Duck™ cartoon called – wait for it – *Trick or Treat*.

The movie *Halloween* was a low budget blockbuster. In fact, it took only three weeks to film. Ironically, the legendary mask was a reworking of one of the few masks they could find at the last minute – the mask of *Star Trek* captain, *T.J Hooker* star, and *Priceline* host, William Shatner.

Six Must Watch Movies on Halloween

- Dracula (1931 version)
- Frankenstein (1931 version)
- The Wolf Man (1941 version)
- The Mummy (1932 version)
- The Bride of Frankenstein (1835 version)
- Abbott and Costello Meet Frankenstein (1948)

The custom of trick-or-treating for Unicef – to gather spare change for the United Nation's children's fund – began in 1950. A family in Philadelphia collected spare change while trick-or-treating. They decided to give the money to Unicef to help children in the wake of World War II who were in need of help. The following year, children across the United States were collecting money while trick-or-treating. In 1959, Lassie helped advertise the collection boxes on their first TV campaign. And in 1967 President Lyndon Johnson declared October 31 National Unicef Day (in perpetuity). By 2010, the trick-or-treaters had collected more than $160 million since its inception in 1950.

Monster Mash by Bobby "Boris" Pickett
Facts

1. *Monster Mash*, that popular song, actually came out in August 1962.

2. The song was on an LP called "The Original Monster Mash"

3. The song reached Number 1 on the Billboard Hot 100 chart on October 20…..which made it popular just in time for Halloween.

4. The sound of the coffin in the song was made by pulling a rusty nail out of a board. And that bubbling cauldron??? It was bubbles being blown into water.

5. The song was inspired in part by the Mashed Potato, a dance that was popular at the time.

6. The Crypt-Kickers performed the song with Pickett.

HALLOWEEN EXTRAS

Hey, don't fear if your child digs in to many pieces of chocolate following Halloween. Chocolate contains tannin which inhibits the production of bacteria. Along with that, chocolate tends to be easy to rinse out of the mouth.

The average age for trick-or-treaters is 5 to 13. Typically, in the United Sates, about 36 million kids could be trick-or-treaters on any given Halloween. Given the fact that 93 percent of children go trick-or-treating, there are going to be a lot of trick-or-treaters. Got candy?

The top two Halloween costumes for kids are – princesses and witches.

The top two Halloween costumes for adults are – witches and pirates

Costumes aren't just for people. About ten percent of people also dress their pets for the black and orange holiday. Jinkies Scooby™!

In some parts of the United States, Halloween has taken on its own nickname. People (not all, mind you) in parts of Ohio, Massachusetts, New Hampshire, New York, and Iowa actually dub it "beggar's night." It is connected to the idea that kids are "begging" for treats.

Halloween Treats. Here is a list of must haves for Halloween

- Pumpkin Pie
- Candy Corn
- Candy Apples
- Caramel Apples
- Pumpkin Pie Seeds

Not everyone likes the idea of "trick or treating" as a concept....particularly the ceremonial trick part. Some cultures remove the whole trick part altogether. In Scotland, kids usually ask something like, "The Sky Is Blue the Grass Is Green, May We Have Our Halloween!"

Guising, the original name for trick-or-treating, dates back to when revelers went door to door in costume, asking for food or money.

Most pagans did not believe devils or ogres or monster posed a danger on Halloween. They worried that fairies might be after them for taking over much of the fairy land. Fairies were often said to cause trouble on Halloween night.

Party time. Want to host a hit party? Halloween is a sure bet. It is the third most popular partying day, after New Years Eve and Super Bowl Sunday.

It is believed that the first Halloween cards were sent in 1908. And, the most popular card….none other than the grandparent to grandchild variety.

Other names for Halloween in history…

All Hallow's Eve
Hell's Night
Lamswool
Nutcrack Night
Samhain
San-Apple Night
Snap Apple Night
Summer's End
Witches's Night
Beggar's Night

IT HAPPENED ON HALLOWEEN

In 1926, magician Harry Houdini died in Detroit. He passed away having suffered from a ruptured appendix days before caused by a fan who punched him – Harry liked to show off his ability to "take punches" but was caught unprepared. He was interested in the spirit world and vowed to contact his family on Halloween if he could find a way. So far, he has not, though many attempts have been made to contact him.

Come on down! On October 31, 2006, legendary game show host Bob Barker retired from the *Price is Right* after 35 years of hosting the show. He hosted his first show on September 4, 1972.

My! What big eyes you have! On October 31, 1941, the legendary monument, Mount Rushmore, was completed. It was designed to have a large hall of record placed inside it, to hold famous American documents. Money ran out to do this, so it has a small vault with copies of famous documents inside it instead.

Word Search

Try to find the following Halloween words in this word search.

c	t	m	u	m	m	y	t	g	s
t	b	w	v	a	m	d	r	k	h
y	a	s	d	c	v	g	t	c	a
o	c	b	u	m	a	s	m	m	u
y	m	m	a	t	m	u	o	u	n
d	v	a	d	a	p	c	h	m	t
n	w	i	t	c	h	g	g	p	n
a	i	r	o	m	c	a	m	r	x
c	v	a	m	p	i	r	e	k	n
s	d	p	u	m	p	k	i	n	b

bat   candy   cat   ghost   haunt
mummy   pumpkin   vampire   witch

Word Search Answers

		m	u	m	m	y			
t									h
	a						t		a
		b					s		u
y				t			o		n
d				a			h		t
n	w	i	t	c	h		g		
a									
c	v	a	m	p	i	r	e		
		p	u	m	p	k	i	n	

The horses have it. On October 31, 1917, the Battle of Beersheba was fought. It marked the last time a cavalry successfully launched an attack. The attack happened as part of the battles in the Sinai Peninsula during World War I. The Australian Fourth Light Brigade led the cavalry charge. The end result was a British victory over the Ottoman and German soldiers.

Oh schism! On October 31, 1517, religious founder Martin Luther marched to Wittenburg and nailed his 95 theses on the Wittenburg Church. Little did he know at the time he was starting a revolution.

Going for silver. In 1864, Nevada was admitted to the United States. What a boon for silver prices....and the TV show *Bonanza*™. Incidentally, it was admitted as a state in a rushed effort. The elections of 1864 were held on November 8 of that year and the admission of Nevada would help ensure Abraham Lincoln was re-elected.

In 843, the first All Hallow's Eve was held on October 31. The Catholic holiday was celebrated to help merge pagan and Christian beliefs while honoring Christian saints.

Famous People Born on Halloween
- John Keats – doctor turned poet, in 1785
- Boston Custer – George Armstrong's younger brother was born in 1848. He was with Custer and died at the Battle of Little Big Horn
- Juliette Gordon Low – founder of the Girl Scouts, was born in 1860
- Dale Rogers – cowgirl and wife of famous cowboy Roy Rogers, was born in 1912
- Michael Collins – the astronaut and often forgotten man of Apollo 11, who stayed in the orbiter while Neil Armstrong and Edwin Aldrin walked on the moon, was born in 1930.
- Dan Rather – the famous CBS journalist, was born in 1931
- Eugene Orowitz – born in 1936, this track star turned actor would later change his name to Mihcael Landon
- Willow Smith – actress, singer, and daughter of Will Smith and Jada Pinckett Smith, was born in 2000.

Legend of Sleepy Hollow
Background on the story

The Legend of Sleepy Hollow by
Washington Irving has long been a popular
tale. The story itself has a great vignette of
an early American Halloween. While the
story is fiction, there are elements based on
reality. Historians believe that the tale is
based on a German folktale set in New
York. Ichabod Crane is likely based on a
soldier that author Washington Irving met.
Likewise, Eleanor Van Tassel, a resident of
Sleepy Hollow, may have been the
inspiration for Katrina Van Tassel. The
graves of Van Tassel family members and
Ichabod Crane can be seen in Sleepy
Hollow. And, the bridge that Ichabod Crane
crosses is believed to be the bridge that
crossed Pocantico River.

Happy Halloween!

Have a happy and safe holiday.

Remember if you are going out, be careful on the streets, wear light clothing, and carry a flashlight.

And if you are an adult, don't scare the kids, give good candy, and try to use artificial lights in the pumpkins.

Trick or treat!

And thanks for reading!

Resources

"The Economics of Halloween" URL:
http://www.creditloan.com/infographics/the-economics-of-halloween/

"Facts About Halloween." URL:
http://www.todayifoundout.com/index.php/2010/10/15-facts-about-halloween/

Facts About Halloween
http://www.facts-about.org.uk/facts-about-halloween.htm

Forty Fun Facts About Halloween
http://facts.randomhistory.com/halloween-facts.html

Halloween Fact or Fiction. Halloween Alliance
URL: http://halloweenalliance.com/halloween/halloween-fact-fiction.htm

URL: History.com. "Halloween"
http://www.history.com/topics/halloween

History. Com "History of Halloween."
http://www.history.com/topics/history-of-trick-or-treating

National Geographic.com
http://news.nationalgeographic.com/news/2008/10/081027-halloween-facts-costumes-history_2.html

Pumpkin Masters
http://www.pumpkinmasters.com/halloween-facts.asp

"Top Ten Halloween Songs"
http://www.billboard.com/features/the-top-10-halloween-songs-1005445412.story#/features/the-top-10-halloween-songs-1005445412.story

www.ingramcontent.com/pod-product-compliance
Lightning Source LLC
Chambersburg PA
CBHW072314290526

45794CB00002B/654